AF280300

More Visibility and Empowerment for Introverts

Unlock the hidden potential in your team

Christian Mueller, MSc.

Impressum

Bibliografische Information der Deutschen Nationalbibliothek:
Die Deutsche Nationalbibliothek verzeichnet diese Publikation in der
Deutschen Nationalbibliografie; detaillierte bibliografische Daten sind im
Internet über http://dnb.dnb.de abrufbar.

© 2025 Christian Müller

Verlag: BoD · Books on Demand, Überseering 33, 22297 Hamburg,
bod@bod.de
Druck: Libri Plureos GmbH, Friedensallee 273, 22763 Hamburg

ISBN: 978-3-7597-8852-8

Content

INTRODUCTION

Ladies and gentlemen, it's time to give introverts the respect and recognition they deserve! For too long, the quiet and reflective among us have been overlooked and undervalued in a world that often celebrates the loudest and most outgoing personalities. But that is all about to change.

This book is about Diversity. Does this sound strange to you? Of course, Diversity is often framed to gender, ethnicity, age, and disability diversity. But there is more. Diversity is also about different personalities. People with different psychological typology attributes have different views of the world and how the world is working. (Kuřetová, 2010) This book will help you as a Leader or HR Person to give introverts the visibility and empowerment they need. Don't oversee these valuable Members of your team again in the next Talent Discussion. "More Visibility and Empowerment for Introverts" is a must-read for anyone who cares about unlocking the true potential of their teams.

As a leader or HR professional, you know better than anyone that every individual brings unique skills and strengths to the table. And yet, despite this knowledge, introverts are all too often left out in the cold. They may be overlooked for promotions, passed over for important projects, or simply dismissed as "not leadership material."

But what if I told you that introverts possess a wealth of untapped potential that could be harnessed to transform your organization? What if I told you that by giving them the right tools and opportunities, introverts could emerge as some of your most valuable and innovative team members?

That's exactly what "More Visibility and Empowerment for Introverts" aims to achieve. This book is contents practical strategies and actionable tips for creating a workplace culture that values and celebrates introverts.

You'll learn how to create more inclusive meetings, foster better communication between introverts and extroverts, and help introverted team members step up and take on leadership roles. You'll also discover how to tap into the unique strengths of introverts, such as their ability to think deeply, and creatively, and use these qualities to drive innovation and growth.

But this book isn't just about helping introverts succeed. It's about creating a workplace culture that values diversity and inclusivity in all its forms. It's about recognizing that different people bring different perspectives and strengths to the table and that by embracing these differences, we can create a more resilient, dynamic, and successful organization.

So, if you are ready to take your leadership skills to the next level, and unlock the full potential of your team, then "More Visibility and Empowerment for Introverts" is the book for you. With its groundbreaking insights, practical advice, and inspiring stories of introverts who have succeeded against the odds, this is a book that will change the way you think about leadership and HR forever.

Preliminary comment

In the following chapters, I am using statements and classifications. Here it is important to note that classification into boxes is not to be seen as a fact. Rather, it is individual characteristics that can apply. The absolute pure form is rarely found, but rather one of the many mixed forms and shades. Likewise, I would like to clarify that neither an extroverted nor an introverted expression of a personality is better or worse. All personalities have their justifications and can be successful.

CHAPTER 1
UNDERSTANDING INTROVERSION

"There's zero correlation between being the best talker and having the best ideas." - Susan Cain

When you think of an introvert, what comes to mind? Many people may conjure up images of quiet, reserved, and shy individuals. While these stereotypes may have some truth to them, they only scratch the surface of what it means to be an introvert. Introverts often get a bad reputation, but they possess many valuable traits that can benefit individuals and organizations alike.

At its core, introversion is a personality trait that describes how someone interacts with the world around them. Introverts are individuals who tend to be more reflective, introspective, and reserved in social situations. They often prefer to work independently and may find large group settings overwhelming or draining. But despite these tendencies, introverts possess a wealth of unique strengths that make them invaluable members of any team.

Introverts thrive in solitude, and they often find that they perform their best work when they are alone. Solitude allows them to focus on their thoughts and ideas, without the distractions of the outside world. In a world that is constantly connected and busy, solitude has become a rare commodity. However, introverts understand the value of taking time for themselves, and they make it a priority to recharge their energy through solitude.

So why should you care about introversion?

Despite the common belief that extroverted qualities are essential for success; the truth is that some of the most successful people in the world are introverts. From Bill Gates to Warren Buffett to J.K. Rowling, introverts have been quietly achieving greatness for years.

Unfortunately, we often associate success with extroverted qualities such as being outgoing, assertive, and charismatic. This leads many introverts to feel like they must change who they are to fit in and succeed in the workplace.

If we talk about introverts. It is not talking about a minority. It is estimated that around 50 percent of the whole U.S. working population can be counted as introverts. (Smith, 2018).

Understanding the neuroscience behind introversion

Introversion has long been a subject of fascination and debate among psychologists, sociologists, and business leaders. However, it is only in recent years that scientists have begun to uncover the fascinating neuroscience behind this personality trait.

Recent studies have shown that these preferences are not just a matter of personal taste, but they are also reflected in differences in the way the brain processes information. For example, one study published in the journal Frontiers in Human Neuroscience found that introverts and extroverts differ in the way their brains respond to rewards. Researchers found that extroverts tend to be more motivated by rewards that involve social interaction or excitement, while introverts are more motivated by rewards that involve quiet reflection or introspection.

Another study, published in the Journal of Neuroscience, found that introverts tend to have a higher level of activity in the prefrontal cortex, which is the area of the brain responsible for planning, decision-making, and self-reflection. This heightened activity in the prefrontal cortex may help explain why introverts tend to be more thoughtful and deliberate in their decision-making than extroverts.

Studies have found that introverts tend to have a stronger response to sensory stimulation, such as loud noises or bright lights. This heightened sensitivity can make them feel overwhelmed in busy environments, which is why they often seek out quiet spaces where they can focus their attention.

So, what does all this mean for introverts in the workplace?

It is simply a different way of processing information and experiencing the world. Businesses can offer quiet spaces or flexible working hours for introverted employees who prefer to work independently or in a low-stimulation environment. They can also provide opportunities for introverted employees to engage in deep, focused work, such as research or analysis, which plays to their strengths.

Furthermore, businesses can encourage introverted employees to take breaks and recharge their batteries when they feel overwhelmed or overstimulated. This can include offering mindfulness or meditation sessions or simply encouraging employees to take a walk outside to clear their minds.

The neuroscience behind introversion is a fascinating and rapidly evolving field of study. By understanding the way, the brain processes information and responds to stimuli, we can gain a deeper appreciation for the unique strengths and challenges of introverts.

Types of Introverts

As human beings, we all possess unique personality traits that make us who we are. Some of us are outgoing and social, while others prefer solitude and quiet reflection. For those who fall into the latter category, they may identify as an introvert. But did you know that there are different types of introverts? Introverts differ from each other, and you may mistake one for another, let's explore a few:

- **The Quiet Ones: Shy Introverts**
  Shy introverts are often misunderstood as snubs or aloof. In reality, they simply feel more comfortable in their own company or with a few close friends. They tend to be sensitive and empathetic individuals who may struggle with social anxiety. They may need extra time to recharge after social

interactions and may prefer to express themselves through writing or other creative outlets.

- **The Daydreamers: Imaginative Introverts**
Imaginative introverts are often lost in their own thoughts and inner worlds. They may have a rich inner life and a vivid imagination and may be drawn to creative pursuits such as writing, art, or music. They may also struggle with practical tasks and may need extra support in organizing their thoughts and ideas.

- **The Analyzers: Thoughtful Introverts**
Thoughtful introverts are often deep thinkers who enjoy exploring complex ideas and concepts. They may have a keen sense of observation and may be skilled at analyzing patterns and trends. They may prefer to spend their time in quiet contemplation or engage in intellectual pursuits such as reading or research.

In addition to their analytical strengths, thoughtful introverts are often highly sensitive to their environment and can pick up on subtle mood changes. This sensitivity can make them adept at reading people and situations, which can be valuable in leadership roles. They may also be skilled at creating a peaceful and productive work environment, as they are attuned to the needs of those around them. Their combination of analytical abilities and sensitivity can make them effective and empathetic leaders who can inspire and motivate their team members.

- **The Secret Keepers: Private Introverts**
  Private introverts are often guarded and may struggle with vulnerability. They may be selective about whom they open up to and may prefer to keep their thoughts and feelings to themselves. They may be introspective and reflective and may enjoy spending time in nature or engaging in activities that allow them to connect with their inner selves.

- **The Rebels: Independent Introverts**
  Independent introverts are often self-reliant and may be drawn to unconventional paths in life. They may resist authority and may prefer to forge their own path rather than follow the crowd. They may be passionate about causes they believe in and may be willing to take risks to pursue their goals.

- **The Empaths: Sensitive Introverts**
  Sensitive introverts are often highly attuned to the emotions of others. They may be skilled at reading body language and may have a deep sense of empathy for those around them. They may be drawn to careers in counseling, social work, or other fields where they can use their skills to help others.

- **The Adventurers: Social Introverts**
  Social introverts may seem like an oxymoron, but they do exist! These individuals enjoy socializing and may have a

wide circle of friends, but they also need
time alone to recharge. They may be skilled
at navigating social situations and may have
a strong sense of humor and wit.

- **The Visionaries: Creative Introverts**
  Creative introverts are often artists, writers,
  musicians, or other creative types. They
  may have a unique perspective on the world
  and may use their creativity to express
  themselves and connect with others. They
  may struggle with self-doubt and may need
  extra support in pursuing their passions.

- **The Seekers: Spiritual Introverts**
  Spiritual introverts may be drawn to
  contemplative practices such as meditation,
  yoga, or prayer. They may have a deep
  sense of connection to the universe and
  may be skilled at sensing subtle energies.
  They may be drawn to spirituality and may
  seek out ways to connect with their higher
  selves.

It's important to recognize that there are different types of introverts, each with their own unique strengths and challenges. An individual may possess one or more types of introversion, and this can lead to internal conflicts and challenges in navigating social situations and relationships. However, understanding the different types of introverts can help us appreciate and respect the diversity of personalities and behaviors among introverted individuals.

CHAPTER 2
CHALLENGES AND STRENGTHS OF INTROVERTS

"Quiet people have the loudest minds." - Stephen Hawking

Understanding the challenges that introverts face in the workplace

When it comes to the workplace, introverts face a unique set of challenges that are often overlooked. From open office layouts to team-building activities, the workplace can sometimes feel like it's designed for extroverts, leaving introverts feeling left out and misunderstood.

One of the biggest challenges that introverts face in the workplace is the pressure to constantly engage in social interactions. This can include everything from casual chit-chat to after-work happy hours, and it can be exhausting for introverts who thrive in solitude and quiet spaces. While extroverts may find these social interactions energizing, introverts often find them draining, which can lead to feelings of burnout and overwhelm.

Another challenge that introverts face in the workplace is the expectation to speak up and assert themselves in meetings and group settings. While introverts may have valuable insights and ideas to contribute, they may not feel comfortable sharing them in a group setting, especially if they feel like they are being overshadowed by more extroverted colleagues. This can lead to introverts feeling like their contributions are not valued, which can be demotivating and disheartening.

Open office layouts can also be a challenge for introverts. While these layouts are often designed to encourage collaboration and communication, they can also be overwhelming for introverts who thrive in quiet, private spaces. Without a designated workspace to call their own, introverts may feel like they don't have a safe haven to retreat to when they need to recharge their energy.

Another challenge for introverts in the workplace is the pressure to participate in team-building activities. While these activities can be a great way to build and strengthen relationships, they can also be uncomfortable for introverts who may feel like they are being forced to engage in activities that are outside of their comfort zone.

Debunking common misconceptions about introverts

Misconceptions about introverts are widespread, and they can lead to misunderstandings and missed opportunities in the workplace. As a result, it's essential to debunk these misconceptions and understand introverts for who they are.

One of the most common misconceptions about introverts is that they are shy and socially awkward. While it's true that some introverts may struggle with social interactions, this is not a defining characteristic of all introverts. In fact, many introverts are skilled communicators and have excellent social skills. They simply prefer to spend more time in quieter, low-stimulation environments, which allows them to recharge and process their thoughts.

Another common misconception is that introverts don't enjoy working in teams or collaborating with others. This couldn't be further from the truth. Introverts can work well in teams and can be excellent collaborators. However, they may prefer to work in smaller groups or with individuals they feel comfortable with. When introverts are given the space and time to contribute in their own way, they can bring unique perspectives and ideas to the table.

Some people also believe that introverts are not suited for leadership roles because they are too reserved or not assertive enough. However, introverts can make excellent leaders. They often excel at listening and observing, which allows them to pick up on subtle cues and nuances that others may miss. Additionally, introverts tend to be thoughtful and reflective, which can lead to more deliberate decision-making and strategic planning. By empowering introverts to take on leadership roles, organizations can benefit from their valuable insights and approaches.

Another common misconception is that introverts are not as successful as extroverts. However, this is simply not true. Many highly successful individuals, from business leaders to artists to scientists, are introverts.

Instead of viewing introverts as a liability or a hindrance, we can embrace their strengths and empower them to contribute in meaningful ways. Introverts are capable of acting like extroverts for the sake of work they consider important, people they love, or anything they value highly. When introverts are given the space and support they need to thrive, everyone benefits.

Exploring the unique strengths that introverts bring to the table

As we have discussed the challenges that introvert face in the workplace, it's crucial to recognize that they also bring a plethora of unique strengths that can significantly benefit any organization. It is essential to note that not all introverts will possess these strengths equally, but their potential to contribute positively to the workplace is undeniable.

Here are eight of the key strength's introverts can bring to the table:

1. One of the key strengths of introverts is their ability to think deeply, analyze complex issues and arrive at thoughtful solutions. While extroverts may thrive in a fast-paced, multitasking environment, introverts tend to perform best when they can concentrate on one thing at a time. This ability to immerse

themselves fully in a task can lead to high-quality work and innovative solutions.

2. Introverts tend to be excellent listeners and observers, able to pick up on details that others may miss. There is a certain magic in the way introverts listen. They don't just hear the words that are spoken, but they also pick up on the subtle tones and hidden meanings that are often missed by extroverts. It is this ability to truly understand what others are saying that gives introverts a unique advantage in the workplace. When an introvert listens, they create a space for the speaker to feel heard and validated. They give their full attention, with an open mind and heart. They don't interrupt or rush to offer their own opinion, but instead, they allow the speaker to fully express themselves.

   This kind of listening creates an atmosphere of trust and respect. When people feel heard, they are more likely to be open and honest, which can lead to more productive conversations and deeper connections. Introverted listening also has the power to transform relationships. When introverts listen to their colleagues, they create a bond and show that they care and are willing to support their colleagues in a meaningful way.

3. Introverts are also often excellent at working independently and focusing on complex, detail-oriented tasks. Because they are less likely to be distracted by social interaction or external stimuli, introverts can often stay focused for longer periods and dive deeper into complex projects. This can make them particularly valuable in roles that require deep analytical skills or attention to detail, such as research, data analysis, or software development.

4. Introverts have deep empathy and compassion for others, often serving as a beacon of calm and understanding in chaotic times.

5. Introverts understand the value of preparation, and they often spend more time planning and strategizing than their extroverted counterparts. In a workplace, the power of preparation can lead to greater success and less stress. Introverts are able to anticipate challenges and create contingency plans, which allows them to remain calm and focused in the face of adversity.

6. Introverts have a natural curiosity and a love for learning. They are always seeking new knowledge and information, and they enjoy diving deep into a topic to gain a deeper understanding. In a workplace, the joy of learning can lead to innovation. Introverts are able to bring new ideas and perspectives to the table, and their thirst for knowledge can lead to breakthroughs and advancements in their field.

7. Introverts understand the importance of setting boundaries, both for themselves and

for others. They know their limits and can communicate them effectively, which allows them to maintain a healthy work-life balance. In a workplace, boundaries are important for preventing burnout and maintaining mental health. Introverts are able to recognize when they need to step back and take a break, and they are able to communicate their needs to their colleagues and superiors.

8. Finally, introverts often have a natural inclination toward creativity and innovation. Because they spend so much time reflecting on their thoughts and ideas, introverts are often able to come up with unique solutions and perspectives that others may not have considered. In addition, introverts often have a strong appreciation for beauty and aesthetics, which can make them particularly valuable in roles that require creative problem-solving, such as advertising or design.

CHAPTER 3
CREATING AN INCLUSIVE WORKPLACE CULTURE

"True inclusion is not about fitting in, it's about belonging. Inclusion is not simply making room at the table; it's about creating a space where everyone has a voice and feels valued." - Mellody Hobson

Diversity and inclusivity are more than just buzzwords. They are essential ingredients for business success in today's rapidly evolving global marketplace. Companies that embrace diversity and inclusivity are more likely to attract and retain top talent, create a more innovative and creative workforce, and ultimately, achieve greater financial success.

But why is diversity and inclusivity so important, and how can businesses harness the power of these principles to drive growth and success?

Diversity and inclusivity are essential for attracting and retaining top talent. In today's competitive job market, skilled workers have their pick of employers. If a company wants to stand out and attract the best and brightest, it needs to create a workplace culture that values diversity and inclusivity. This means creating a culture where people of all backgrounds and identities feel welcome, valued, and respected. When employees feel that their unique perspectives and experiences are valued, they are more likely to feel engaged, committed, and invested in their work. In turn, this leads to higher productivity, lower turnover, and greater overall job satisfaction.

In addition to attracting and retaining top talent, diversity and inclusivity can also fuel innovation and creativity. When people from different backgrounds and with different perspectives come together to solve a problem, they are more likely to arrive at innovative and creative solutions. This is because diverse teams bring a wider range of knowledge, experience, and perspectives to the table. When people are exposed to new and different ways of thinking, they are more likely to challenge their assumptions and come up with new and innovative ideas.

But creating a truly inclusive workplace culture is not always easy. It requires a concerted effort to overcome biases and create a culture of respect and acceptance. One key strategy for promoting diversity and inclusivity is to actively seek out diverse perspectives and experiences. This can be done through targeted recruiting efforts, mentorship programs, and employee resource groups. By intentionally seeking out diverse perspectives and experiences, companies can create a culture where everyone feels valued and included.

Another key strategy for promoting diversity and inclusivity is to provide training and education for employees. This can include workshops on unconscious bias, diversity and inclusion, and cultural competency. When employees understand the importance of diversity and inclusivity, they are more likely to value and embrace it in their day-to-day work.

It is important to create a culture where everyone feels comfortable speaking up and sharing their perspectives. This means creating a culture of psychological safety, where employees feel that they can speak up without fear of retaliation or judgment. This can be achieved by creating open lines of communication, encouraging feedback and suggestions, and valuing the contributions of every employee.

How to create a workplace culture that values introverts and extroverts alike

As leaders, it is our responsibility to create workplace cultures that value and celebrate the unique qualities of all our team members, regardless of whether they are introverted or extroverted. The truth is, introverts and extroverts have different ways of engaging with the world, and each has its own set of strengths and challenges. By creating a workplace culture that values and embraces both, we can unlock the full potential of our teams and drive success for our businesses.

Here are some practical steps that you can take to create a workplace culture that values both introverts and extroverts:

1. **Recognize and celebrate differences:** The first step to creating a workplace culture that values both introverts and extroverts is to

acknowledge and celebrate the differences between the two. As leaders, we need to recognize that introverts and extroverts have different ways of processing information, communicating, and engaging with others.

2. **Provide opportunities for individual and group work:** Introverts tend to excel at individual work, while extroverts thrive in group settings. By providing opportunities for both individual and group work, we can create a workplace culture that allows both introverts and extroverts to play to their strengths. This might mean providing quiet spaces for introverts to work, while also facilitating collaborative spaces for extroverts to brainstorm and work together.

3. **Emphasize active listening:** Active listening is an essential skill for any workplace culture, but it's particularly important when it comes to valuing

introverts. Introverts tend to be more thoughtful and deliberate in their communication and may take longer to process and respond to information. By emphasizing active listening, we can create a workplace culture that allows introverts the space they need to fully articulate their thoughts and ideas.

4. **Encourage diverse perspectives:** By creating a workplace culture that values and encourages diverse perspectives, we can foster an environment that values both introverts and extroverts. This might mean actively seeking out opinions and ideas from team members with different communication styles and personalities and creating space for all team members to share their thoughts and ideas.

5. **Provide opportunities for reflection and feedback:** Introverts tend to be more reflective and introspective than extroverts

and may need more time to process feedback and information. By providing opportunities for reflection and feedback, we can create a workplace culture that values the unique qualities of introverts. This might mean scheduling regular check-ins with team members to provide feedback and support or providing opportunities for individual reflection and goal-setting.

6. **Lead by example:** As leaders, we have a responsibility to model the behaviors and values that we want to see in our workplace cultures. This might mean actively seeking out input and feedback from team members with different communication styles or modeling active listening and reflective behaviors.

Practical strategies for promoting inclusivity in your organization

Building a culture of inclusivity in the workplace is not just a "feel-good" initiative. It is a fundamental aspect of creating a successful and sustainable organization. When employees feel valued, respected, and included, they become more invested in their work, more productive, and more likely to remain committed to the organization for the long term.

1. Start with education and awareness

Before you can create a truly inclusive workplace, you need to understand what that means and how it looks in practice. Start by educating yourself and your team on the importance of diversity and inclusion, as well as the different forms of bias and discrimination that can exist in the workplace. Consider offering training and workshops on topics such as unconscious bias, microaggressions, and cultural awareness.

2. Encourage open communication

One of the most important aspects of creating an inclusive workplace is encouraging open communication. Employees should feel comfortable sharing their thoughts and experiences without fear of judgment or retribution. Make sure you have a feedback system in place that allows employees to share their opinions and ideas. This could be in the form of regular check-ins, anonymous surveys, or an open-door policy.

3. Emphasize the value of diversity

Inclusivity is not just about meeting quotas or checking boxes. It is about recognizing the value that different perspectives and experiences can bring to the table. Emphasize the importance of diversity in your organization and make sure everyone understands the benefits of a diverse team. Encourage employees to share their own unique perspectives and experiences and create opportunities for cross-functional collaboration.

4. Create a culture of respect

Respect is a fundamental aspect of creating an inclusive workplace. Make sure all employees are treated with respect and dignity, regardless of their race, gender, sexual orientation, or any other factor. This includes not tolerating any form of discrimination, harassment, or bullying. Make it clear that this behavior will not be tolerated and provide resources for employees who experience or witness such behavior.

5. Be open to feedback and change

Creating an inclusive workplace isn't a one-and-done task. It requires ongoing effort and a willingness to adapt and change. Be open to feedback from employees and make changes as needed. This could include revisiting policies and procedures, creating new initiatives, or adjusting the company culture. The key is to remain flexible and open-minded.

6. Celebrate diversity and inclusion

Finally, don't forget to celebrate diversity and inclusion in your workplace. Recognize and celebrate the accomplishments of employees from all backgrounds and make sure everyone feels valued and appreciated. This could include highlighting diverse achievements in company-wide communications, hosting diversity-themed events or celebrations, or creating affinity groups or employee resource groups.

Promoting inclusivity in your organization requires effort, education, and a willingness to change. By creating a culture of respect, encouraging open communication, and celebrating diversity, you can create a workplace that values all employees and promotes success for everyone. Remember, diversity isn't just a buzzword - it's essential for creating a thriving and successful organization.

CHAPTER 4

COMMUNICATION STRATEGIES FOR INTROVERTS AND EXTROVERTS

Effective communication is not about being loud or soft-spoken, but about finding the right words and the right approach that resonates with your audience.

By understanding and embracing our communication styles as introverts and extroverts, we can create a more harmonious and productive workplace, where ideas flow freely, and everyone feels heard and valued. It is a common misconception that extroverts are better communicators than introverts. The truth is that both introverts and extroverts have unique communication styles that should be understood and appreciated to create a truly inclusive workplace.

As I have said before, communication is not just about speaking, it is about listening and understanding. Extroverts tend to communicate by speaking out loud and expressing their thoughts and ideas in a clear and direct manner. They are often comfortable speaking in front of large groups of people and enjoy networking and socializing.

On the other hand, Introverts have a communication style that is more reflective and measured. They tend to internalize their thoughts before speaking, which can lead to more thoughtful and insightful contributions. As active listeners, introverts often pick up on nuances that may escape others, making them an asset to any team. However, introverts may require more time to formulate their responses and may prefer to communicate in writing rather than in person.

To create a workplace culture that values both introverts and extroverts, it is important to understand and appreciate these communication differences.

Practical tips for bridging the communication gap between these two personality types

There are significant differences in communication styles between introverts and extroverts. It is essential to bridge this gap to promote inclusivity and productivity in the workplace. We will explore some practical tips for bridging the communication gap between these two personality types.

1. Listen with intent

One of the most significant differences between introverts and extroverts is the way they process information. Extroverts tend to process information externally, meaning they prefer to think out loud and verbally process information. Introverts, on the other hand, tend to process information internally and prefer to think things through before sharing their thoughts. As a result, introverts may take longer to respond or may seem quiet in group discussions.

To bridge this communication gap, it's important to listen with intent. When an introvert is speaking, give them the time and space they need to express their thoughts fully. Avoid interrupting or finishing their sentences. Similarly, when an extrovert is speaking, allow them to verbalize their thoughts and work through ideas out loud.

2. Avoid assumptions

It's easy to assume that someone's communication style is indicative of their personality type. However, this can be a dangerous assumption to make. Not all introverts are shy and reserved, and not all extroverts are outgoing and talkative. Avoid making assumptions about someone's communication style based on their personality type, and instead, focus on their individual communication preferences.

3. Adapt your communication style

To bridge the communication gap between introverts and extroverts, it's essential to adapt your communication style. For example, if you're an extrovert, you may need to slow down and allow introverts to process information before responding. You may also need to provide more time for introverts to prepare for meetings or presentations.

On the other hand, if you're an introvert, you may need to step out of your comfort zone and speak up more in group discussions. You may also need to practice being more concise and direct in your communication to ensure that your message is heard and understood.

4. Provide multiple communication channels

Introverts tend to prefer written communication, while extroverts prefer verbal communication. To bridge this communication gap, it's important to provide multiple communication channels. This could include email, instant messaging, and video conferencing in addition to in-person meetings and phone calls. By providing multiple communication channels, you can ensure that everyone has the opportunity to communicate in a way that feels comfortable for them.

How to create an environment where all team members feel comfortable speaking up

I don't care if you're working on a rocket ship or just trying to build a successful business, you need everyone's input to make it happen.

First things first, you have to lead by example. If you're not willing to speak up and share your own ideas, how can you expect anyone else to? So, don't be afraid to share your thoughts and be vulnerable with your team. Show them that it's okay to take risks and make mistakes.

It is important to start with "why". This means articulating a clear purpose and vision for the organization and communicating it regularly to all team members. When team members understand why their work matters and how it contributes to the overall mission of the organization, they are more likely to feel invested in the success of the team and be willing to speak up.

Next up, you need to create a safe space for communication. Let your team know that their thoughts and opinions are valuable and that you want to hear them. Encourage open communication, active listening, and constructive feedback. And most importantly, make it clear that there will be no judgment or retaliation for speaking up. This fosters a culture of trust in the team.

What about the naysayers and negative members who are always trying to bring the team down?" Well, here's the thing, if you create an environment where everyone feels valued and heard, those negative folks are definitely going to be outnumbered and outshined by the positivity and creativity of the rest of the team.

Another key to creating an environment where all team members feel comfortable speaking up is to make sure that everyone has a chance to contribute. Don't let the same few people dominate the conversation. Make sure you're giving everyone the opportunity to share their thoughts and ideas. And if someone is quieter or more reserved, take the time to check in with them one-on-one and encourage them to share their thoughts with the group.

Lastly, make sure you're taking action based on the input you receive from your team. Nothing kills a team's morale faster than feeling like their ideas are falling on deaf ears. So, if someone shares an idea or concern, make sure you're taking the time to address it and implement changes if necessary.

CHAPTER 5
EMPOWERING INTROVERTS TO LEAD

"The world needs introverted leaders who are willing to listen, think deeply, and act with conviction. We must empower introverts to step into their leadership potential and show the world what they're capable of."

Are introverts cut out to be leaders? This is a question that has been asked time and time again, yet the answer remains elusive. While it's true that extroverted qualities like charisma and assertiveness have traditionally been valued in leadership roles, there are many successful introverted leaders who prove that introversion and leadership can coexist.

Below are prominent introverted leaders who have made a significant impact in their respective fields:

- **Bill Gates:** A self-identified introvert, has shown that introverts can be very successful leaders and have the potential to achieve great success by leveraging their unique strengths. As the founder of Microsoft, he has achieved tremendous success by utilizing his natural tendency to think deeply and reflect before making decisions. Gates believes that introverts are best suited to use their quiet, introspective nature to their advantage by spending time in solitude, where they can think and read extensively without distraction. This allows them to form well-considered opinions and ideas that can be transformative in the workplace.

  Gates recognizes that introverts may struggle with the social aspects of business, such as networking or pitching ideas to investors. He suggests that introverts should seek out extroverted individuals to help sell their ideas and bring them to the world. By working with others who possess different strengths, introverts can build a team that is both diverse and complementary, allowing them to achieve great success. This approach has proven successful for Gates, who has been able to use his quiet, introspective nature to transform the technology industry while relying on others to help him bring his ideas to fruition.

- **Mark Zuckerberg:** Another introverted leader is not only the founder and CEO of Meta but also a great leader who has revolutionized the way we interact with each other online. While he may come across as aloof, Zuckerberg's leadership style is characterized by his passion for technology and his ability to bring people together to work towards a common goal.

  One of the key factors that make Zuckerberg a great leader is his empathy and concern for his employees. He is known for taking an active interest in the well-being of his team and creating a work environment that is both supportive and challenging. His focus on empowering his employees to take ownership of their work and contribute to the company's success has helped to foster a culture of innovation and collaboration at Meta.

Moreover, Zuckerberg's ability to communicate his vision and inspire his team to work towards it is another key strength that has made him a successful leader. He has a clear understanding of his goals and the steps needed to achieve them, and he is able to communicate these ideas in a way that inspires others to join him. While he may not be the most outgoing or extroverted leader, his thoughtful and deliberate approach to communication has helped him to build trust and respect among his team members. Overall, Mark Zuckerberg's success as a leader is a testament to the fact that introverts can be just as effective in leadership positions as extroverts.

- **Angela Merkel** is one of the most prominent and respected leaders known for her intelligence, strategic thinking, and cool composure. She is also a prime example of a highly successful introverted leader who has channelled her personality traits into greatness.

  As an introvert, Merkel is not the kind of leader who seeks the spotlight or relishes in the limelight. She is not known for her charisma or charm but for her analytical and logical thinking, her attention to detail, and her ability to listen and observe. These are traits that have served her well throughout her career and have enabled her to excel in some of the most challenging and complex roles in politics.

  Merkel's introverted nature has also helped her develop a reputation for being a thoughtful and deliberate decision-maker. She is known for taking her time to weigh all the options, consult with experts, and consider all the possible consequences before making a move. This approach has helped her navigate numerous political crises and challenges that have earned her the nickname "Mutti" (mother) in Germany.

Moreover, Merkel's introverted nature has allowed her to focus on her strengths and develop her skills in areas where introverts often excel, such as analysis, research, and attention to detail. She has a Ph.D. in quantum chemistry and has been praised for her ability to grasp complex scientific and technical issues, which has given her a unique perspective on policy-making and global challenges such as climate change.

Finally, Merkel's introverted personality has enabled her to lead by example and inspire others through her actions rather than her words. She is not a rousing orator or a charismatic speaker, but her quiet determination and steady leadership have earned her the respect and admiration of leaders around the world. She has been instrumental in strengthening the European Union and promoting democracy and human rights globally, and her leadership has been especially critical during the COVID-19 pandemic, where her scientific background and logical approach have helped her guide Germany through this unprecedented crisis.

- **Larry Page:** Despite his introverted personality and geekiness, Larry Page has proven to be an exceptional leader as the co-founder and former CEO of Google. He is known for his ability to think outside the box, his commitment to innovation, and his willingness to take risks. One of the things that set Page apart as a leader is his emphasis on transparency and communication, both with his team and with the wider public.

Page has shared many insights and nuggets of wisdom over the years, including the importance of focusing on long-term goals rather than short-term gains, the need for continual experimentation and iteration, and the value of listening to and learning from others. He has also emphasized the importance of creating a culture of innovation and collaboration, where employees feel empowered to take risks and contribute their ideas. Overall, Page's success as an introverted leader highlights the fact that leadership is not about personality type, but rather about vision, passion, and the ability to inspire and motivate others towards a shared goal.

- **Eleanor Roosevelt:** Popularly called "The introvert who wouldn't keep quiet" is a shining example of a successful introverted leader. Despite her initially shy nature, she went on to become a monumental public figure, giving hundreds of press conferences and speeches throughout her life. As a United Nations delegate, human rights activist, teacher, and lecturer, she averaged 150 speaking engagements a year throughout the 1950s. Her story complicates the idea that introversion and extroversion are dichotomous or the ends of a continuum between which we can locate our true personalities. Rather, her life and career demonstrate how elements of introversion and extroversion can wax, wane, and intermingle over time and depending on environmental circumstances. Roosevelt's journey from a severely shy and withdrawn young person to a public figure with a history of shyness and reclusiveness shows that introversion is not a hindrance to success. It's her ability to overcome her introverted tendencies that makes her a great leader. Through her courage, determination, and willingness to confront her fears, she inspires introverts to follow in her footsteps and pursue their dreams, even if it means stepping out of their comfort zone.

- **Marissa Mayer:** Who served as the CEO of Yahoo! from 2012 to 2017, is widely recognized for her exceptional leadership skills, despite her introverted nature. While her soft-spoken demeanor and reluctance to speak in public may seem at odds with the stereotypical image of a strong and vocal leader, Mayer's unique traits have proven to be key assets in her career.

One of the things that sets Mayer apart as a leader is her technical proficiency. She holds a degree in computer science from Stanford University and was the first female engineer hired by Google. At Yahoo!, she was known for her hands-on approach and deep understanding of the company's products and technologies. Her technical prowess, coupled with her introverted tendencies, allowed her to analyze complex problems and make data-driven decisions, which helped to steer Yahoo! in a more competitive direction.

Another aspect of Mayer's leadership style that stands out is her focus on collaboration. Regardless of her introvert personality, she recognizes the value of building strong relationships with her team members and empowering them to make their own decisions. She is known for fostering a culture of innovation and creativity at Yahoo! and for encouraging her employees to take risks and pursue their ideas.

Mayer's introspective nature also allows her to think deeply about her own leadership style and continuously improve it. She has spoken openly about her shyness and the challenges it has posed for her in the past, but she has also credited it with giving her a unique perspective on leadership. In a 2014 interview with the New York Times, she said, "I've always been a little bit of an introvert, and I think that has helped me to be more analytical and to think things through before I act. It's also made me a good listener, which is a crucial skill for any leader."

Overall, Mayer's introverted nature has allowed her to lead with a thoughtful, analytical approach, foster collaboration, and innovation, and continuously reflect on her own leadership style. These traits have undoubtedly contributed to her success as a leader in the tech industry.

- **JK Rowling:** JK Rowling's incredible success as an author and entrepreneur shows that being an introvert is not a barrier to achieving remarkable things. Many aspects of her introverted nature, such as her deep focus, creativity, and determination, contributed to her success.

One of the most important qualities that make Rowling a good leader is her ability to persevere through adversity. Before she became one of the wealthiest authors in the world, Rowling faced numerous rejections from publishers who didn't believe in her work. She was also a single mother living on welfare, struggling to make ends meet. However, she didn't let these setbacks discourage her and continued to write and submit her manuscript until it was finally accepted.

Another important quality of Rowling's leadership is her empathy and compassion. Her books are known for their themes of acceptance, friendship, and love. Rowling is also known for her creativity and imagination, which are essential qualities for any leader in a creative field. Her ability to craft rich and intricate worlds, characters, and plotlines has captured the imaginations of millions of readers around the world and has led to a massive multimedia franchise that includes movies, theme parks, and merchandise.

Rowling's ability to connect with her audience and inspire them to be their best selves is a testament to her leadership skills. Through her writing and public speaking, she has motivated countless fans to pursue their dreams, believe in themselves, and fight for what they believe in. Her personal story of perseverance, creativity, and empathy has made her a role model for introverts and extroverts alike.

Practical strategies for identifying and developing introverted leaders within your organization

As we have discussed in this book, introverts possess unique qualities that make them excellent leaders. However, identifying and developing introverted leaders within your organization may require some strategic planning and intentional effort.

1. Recognize the strengths of introverted leaders

The first step in identifying and developing introverted leaders is to recognize their strengths. Introverted leaders possess qualities such as deep listening skills, strategic thinking, and the ability to create a calm and focused work environment. These strengths can be invaluable in leadership positions, particularly in industries that require analytical and strategic thinking, such as technology, research, and development.

2. Provide leadership training and development opportunities

Once you have identified potential introverted leaders within your organization, it's essential to provide them with the necessary training and development opportunities to build their leadership skills. This could include leadership workshops, mentorship programs, or executive coaching. These opportunities will not only help them develop their leadership skills but also build their confidence as leaders.

3. Create a leadership development plan

Creating a leadership development plan for introverted leaders is critical. This plan should be tailored to their unique strengths and areas for growth. It should also be developed in collaboration with the introverted leader to ensure that their goals and aspirations are considered. The plan should include specific goals, timelines, and performance metrics to measure progress.

4. Build a supportive network

Introverted leaders often prefer working independently but building a supportive network can be invaluable in their leadership development. This network could include mentors, peers, and colleagues who can provide guidance, support, and feedback. A supportive network can also help introverted leaders build relationships and develop their communication skills.

5. Create an inclusive work environment

Creating an inclusive work environment is critical for developing introverted leaders. This includes fostering a culture of respect, empathy, and understanding. It's essential to recognize that introverted leaders may have different communication styles and work preferences than extroverted leaders. Providing a flexible work environment that allows introverted leaders to work independently or in small groups can help them thrive.

6. Encourage introverted leaders to share their ideas

Encouraging introverted leaders to share their ideas is critical for their leadership development. Introverted leaders may be less likely to speak up in group settings, so it's essential to create opportunities for them to share their thoughts and ideas. This could include one-on-one meetings, brainstorming sessions, or virtual communication channels.

7. Provide opportunities for introverted leaders to highlight their strengths

Providing opportunities for introverted leaders to highlight their strengths can help build their confidence and visibility within the organization.

This could include presenting at conferences, leading projects, or participating in cross-functional teams. These opportunities can also help introverted leaders build relationships and expand their professional networks.

Identifying and developing introverted leaders within your organization requires strategic planning and intentional effort. Recognizing their strengths, providing leadership training and development opportunities, creating a leadership development plan, building a supportive network, creating an inclusive work environment, encouraging introverted leaders to share their ideas, and providing opportunities for them to showcase their strengths are all critical components of this process.

CHAPTER 6
CREATING MORE INCLUSIVE MEETINGS

"Inclusiveness is not just about opening doors for others. It's about creating a world where everyone has the key to unlock their potential."

Why traditional meeting formats can be challenging for Introverts

Traditional meeting formats can be a challenge for introverts. As someone who has studied and written extensively about leadership and communication, I understand why this is the case. In a traditional meeting, extroverted individuals may dominate the conversation, leading to a lack of opportunities for introverts to express their ideas.

This can be particularly challenging for introverts, who often prefer to process information internally before speaking up. In a fast-paced meeting environment, introverts may not have the opportunity to fully develop their thoughts and ideas before the conversation moves on. This can lead to feelings of frustration and a lack of engagement, which can be detrimental to the overall success of the meeting and the organization as a whole.

Additionally, traditional meeting formats often rely on verbal communication, which can be challenging for introverts who prefer written communication. Introverts may struggle to articulate their ideas verbally, which can lead to their ideas getting overlooked or dismissed.

As leaders, it is important to recognize these challenges and create meeting formats that are more conducive to introverts' strengths. One way to do this is by providing ample preparation time before the meeting. This can give introverts the time they need to fully process information and develop their ideas before the meeting begins. Additionally, providing an agenda ahead of time can help introverts prepare and feel more confident about their contributions.

Another strategy is to incorporate more written communication into the meeting. This can include having participants write down their ideas before sharing them verbally or using online collaboration tools that allow participants to contribute to the discussion in real time without the pressure of speaking up in a group setting.

In addition, it is important to create a culture of active listening in meetings. This means actively seeking out and valuing the contributions of all participants, regardless of their communication style. Leaders can model this behavior by actively listening to and incorporating the ideas of introverts in the meeting.

Finally, it's important to provide opportunities for introverts to lead and facilitate meetings. This can allow introverts to play to their strengths, including their ability to listen actively and process information thoroughly. Leaders can identify introverts who have the potential to lead meetings and provide them with the necessary support and training to develop their skills.

Practical strategies for creating more inclusive meeting environments

When it comes to creating more inclusive meeting environments, there are a few key strategies that can help make the experience more comfortable for introverts.

First, it's important to recognize that traditional meeting formats can be challenging for introverts. These formats often prioritize extroverted communication styles, with a focus on rapid-fire discussion and quick decision-making. This can be overwhelming for introverts, who tend to process information more slowly and prefer to take time to reflect before speaking.

To create a more inclusive meeting environment, one strategy is to provide a clear agenda ahead of time. This can help introverts prepare their thoughts and ideas in advance, reducing the pressure of having to think on their feet during the meeting. Additionally, it can be helpful to provide any necessary background information or context ahead of time, so that everyone comes to the meeting with a shared understanding of the topics the meeting will focus on.

Another practical strategy is to use round-robin style discussions, rather than open-floor discussions. In a round-robin format, each person has a set amount of time to speak, without interruption or discussion from others. This can be a more comfortable format for introverts, who may feel more confident and prepared when they know they will have a chance to speak without getting interrupted.

Similarly, using small group discussions or breakout sessions can also be helpful for introverts. This allows for more focused, in-depth discussions in a smaller group setting, rather than a large group discussion where introverts may feel overwhelmed or overshadowed by more extroverted team members.

Finally, it is important to create a culture of active listening and respect for all perspectives. Encourage team members to listen actively and give each other time to speak, without interruption or talking over one another. This can help introverts feel more comfortable sharing their thoughts and ideas, knowing that their contributions are heard and valued by others.

In conclusion, creating more inclusive meeting environments requires a shift away from traditional meeting formats that prioritize extroverted communication styles. By providing clear agendas, using round-robin discussions or small group sessions, and fostering a culture of active listening and respect, organizations can create a more comfortable and productive environment for introverted team members. By embracing the strengths of all team members, regardless of communication style, organizations can create a more inclusive and successful workplace for everyone.

How to ensure that all team members have an equal opportunity to contribute

Creating a workplace environment where all team members have an equal opportunity to contribute is critical for the success of any organization. It is not just a matter of fairness; it is a matter of making the most of the diverse skills and perspectives that each team member brings to the table. However, achieving this level of inclusivity can be a challenge, particularly when a part of the team members may be more introverted or shy than others.

Below are some practical strategies for ensuring that all team members have an equal opportunity to contribute, regardless of their personality type.

Creating a safe and inclusive environment where all team members feel comfortable speaking up is essential. This means fostering a culture of respect and open communication, where everyone's ideas are valued and appreciated. Encourage team members to share their thoughts and ideas and actively listen to what they say. Avoid interrupting or dismissing their contributions, even if you do not necessarily agree with them. Remember, diversity of thought is a powerful asset for any team, and you never know where the next great idea might come from.

Another critical strategy for creating an inclusive meeting environment is to give everyone an equal opportunity to speak. This means being mindful of how you structure meetings and how much time each team member is provided to speak. Consider using a round-robin approach, where each team member is given a set amount of time to talk before moving on to the next person. Alternatively, you could use a "raise your hand" system, where team members can indicate they have something to contribute without interrupting others.

Being mindful of the language and tone used during meetings is also essential. Avoid using overly aggressive or confrontational language, as this can intimidate some team members and discourage them from speaking up. Instead, strive to create a positive and supportive environment where everyone feels comfortable expressing their thoughts and ideas.

It can be helpful to provide opportunities for introverted team members to prepare in advance. Consider sending out an agenda or discussion points before the meeting, giving team members time to reflect on the topics and formulate their thoughts. This can be especially helpful for introverted team members needing more time to process information before sharing their ideas.

Another strategy for creating an inclusive meeting environment is to use visual aids to complement verbal communication. This can be particularly helpful for team members who may be more visual learners or who struggle to express themselves verbally. Consider using whiteboards, diagrams, or charts to illustrate key points and encourage team members to contribute their ideas visually.

CHAPTER 7
CELEBRATING INTROVERTS' SUCCESS

"Introverts often achieve success quietly and without fanfare. Celebrating their accomplishments and recognizing their contributions is important, even if they don't seek the spotlight."

How to recognize and celebrate the achievements of introverted team members

Introverts often prefer to work in the background, avoiding the spotlight and seeking recognition only when they have achieved something remarkable. As leaders, we are responsible for creating a culture where introverted team members feel valued and appreciated and where their contributions are recognized and celebrated.

So, how can we recognize and celebrate the achievements of our introverted team members?

The first step is understanding that introverts are often uncomfortable with public recognition, particularly in large group settings. Instead, they may prefer more intimate and private forms of recognition, such as a handwritten note, a one-on-one conversation, or a small gathering with close colleagues.

It is essential to recognize that introverts may not always be the most vocal about their achievements. They may feel uncomfortable "bragging" about themselves or drawing attention to their successes, and as a result, their contributions may go unnoticed or underappreciated.

To address this, it is important to establish regular check-ins with all team members, regardless of their communication style. This could involve scheduling regular one-on-one meetings or incorporating time for individual updates in team meetings. Giving introverted team members a regular platform to share their successes makes them more likely to feel recognized and valued.

Consider incorporating team-building activities that cater to introverted team members. While traditional team-building activities may involve high-energy group exercises or games, these may not be the most effective way to build camaraderie among introverted team members. Instead, consider activities that allow for more reflection and introspection, such as guided meditations, journaling exercises, or group discussions centered around a shared interest or topic.

Celebrate the achievements of introverted team members in a way that feels authentic and meaningful to them. This could involve highlighting their contributions in a team-wide email, presenting them with a personalized gift or award, or acknowledging their achievements in a way that feels aligned with their values and interests.

CONCLUSION

As leaders and HR professionals, it is time to reassess our approach to our teams. Are we truly valuing and leveraging everyone's unique strengths? Are we creating an inclusive culture that celebrates diversity and encourages everyone to contribute?

The power of introverted leadership is evident. By creating an environment where introverts feel valued, heard, and empowered, we can unleash untapped potential that could drive our organizations to new heights. We must recognize that introverts bring a unique perspective characterized by deep thinking, strategic planning, and a keen awareness of their surroundings.

With the strategies outlined in "More Visibility and Empowerment for Introverts," we can ensure that introverts have an equal opportunity to succeed and thrive in the workplace. By creating more inclusive meeting environments, promoting effective communication between introverts and extroverts, and providing opportunities for introverted team members to take on leadership roles, we can unlock the full potential of our teams.

But this is not just about introverts. This is about creating a workplace culture that values and embraces diversity in all its forms. It is about recognizing that everyone has something valuable to offer, regardless of their personality type or communication style. Creating a culture of appreciation and recognition ensures that everyone feels valued and motivated to do their best work.

So, let's embrace the power of introverted leadership and create a workplace culture that celebrates diversity, inclusivity, and innovation. Let's empower introverts to lead and impact our organizations meaningfully. With the right mindset and tools, anything is possible.

The Author

Christian Mueller has been working in HR management for many years. He completed an apprenticeship as a wholesale and foreign trade merchant. He continued his education to become a Bachelor Professional in Human Resources Management (CCI). He also holds a master's degree in communication and organizational psychology (FHWien WKW). He was trained as a systemic business coach at the University of Applied Sciences in Wismar. His professional career has already taken him to various industries, including wholesale, metal, market research, chemical, and pharmaceutical industries. His professional focus within human resources is on change management, HR organization (structure and reorganization), and corporate culture. He also successfully conducts management training on topics such as The role of a manager, Employee communication, Team leadership, etc., and supports prospective and young managers as a coach in their first steps. He coaches managers and executives in the areas of team leadership and decision-making.

Kuřetová, J. (2010). Managing Diversity in Organisations: A New Approach towards Personality. *International Journal of Diversity in Organizations, Communities, and Nations, 10*(1), 185-194. doi:https://doi.org/10.18848/1447-9532/CGP/v10i01/39809

Smith, D. F. (2018). Mining the Gold That Is Your Introvert Employee. *Journal of Financial Planning, 31*(10), 24-25.